Building a Brand

The Seven Important Steps

By:

James Stevens

Published by Shepal Publishing

Table of Contents

Introduction

Starting your own business is an excellent step to financial freedom. To attain this financial freedom, your business needs to be successful. You may have gone to business school and acquired all the skills that you can to ensure that your operations are smooth, and that you are working with a plan that will lead you to growth and profitability within three or so years. Even with this plan, creating relationships with customers and propelling your business forward could prove challenging. This can all be attributed to having a weak brand.

A brand is an essential component of your business as it ensures that you have an identity that differentiates you from all other similar products in the market. When you have a brand, it becomes easier for you to attain growth over the long term as you can develop your brand with time.

A brand will embody certain aspects of your business, including what your product or service represents, the team that are working for you, and what your business values. It is essential for communicating to both your external audience, as well as those who are working within your business.

To get started with creating your brand, you need to follow the seven distinct steps that are outlined in this book. Doing so will lead you to success, and ensure that at the end of the process, you have an identity for your business that will stand the test of time.

Chapter 1:
The First Step –
Create a Brand Strategy

Your brand needs to have a direction that it is following in the long term to attain success, and for that, you must develop a brand strategy. This strategy should include milestones or goals that you can use to assess whether you are progressing in the right direction. Getting this right when you start will require time and planning, and you will be left with a blueprint for your business. Here's how you can create your brand strategy.

Look at the Big Picture

The first thing that you need to do is figure out what differentiates your brand from all other similar brands. When you are strong in this, you will find that the process of growing your firm becomes much easier. Ask yourself a few questions. Start with the type of firm that you are looking to create. Then consider how you want to grow your firm. When you have this put down clearly, you will find that it is much easier for your brand to grow.

Define your Goal

You need to define your goal so that you are clear about what your brand should represent. This will need you to know what you want to achieve in the long term with your brand, it answers the question of why you have established the brand. Keep in mind that you are not looking at tactics that will help you achieve something in the short term, instead, you want something that will work for you in the long run.

Differentiation

Establish what is different about your product, in comparison to similar products on the market. This difference does not necessarily need to be in the product itself, it could be something that is intangible in nature. Using descriptive words help to further elevate your product, so words like "unique" and "special" can influence the way that the customer views your offering.

To understand how this works, it is best to think about brands that you know and how they have differentiated themselves. What is the first thing that comes to mind with you think of Ferrari? Speed! This means that when you purchase the brand, this is what you are looking for. They have differentiated themselves from other car brands in the market in this way.

Consider Positioning

Think about what the positioning of your brand is going to be considering the product or service that you will be offering. To do this, you need to know what makes your firm different, and the reasons that any potential clients from your target audience would want to work together with you. For this, you will need to create a positioning statement. This statement will normally be between three and five sentences long, and you will capture the overall essence of the position of your brand. Remember to make it realistic, so that you are able to deliver on the promise that you have made.

Understand your Customer

When you do a basic marketing course, you learn how to define your customer based on demographic information such as gender, location and age. When creating your brand strategy, you need to go deeper than that. You need to understand what drives your customer towards your product, their likes and dislikes and overall passions. This will make your customer more real to you as you will understand what they are truly trying to attain from your product or service.

Think of a Strategy in your Message

You need to have a strategy that will build up your message, so that you are able to reach your target audience. When you are crafting your message, keep in mind that you are reaching out to potential clientele and employees, as well as other influential people who may even choose to partner with you. You need to make sure that you have something interesting to express to each of these audiences so that they are better able to relate to your brand. This way, you will be creating a brand that is highly relevant.

Remain Flexible

Your brand strategy is not a contract or a document that is set in stone for your brand development. It is simply an outline or guide which will move you in the right direction. An important aspect of building a brand is maintaining flexibility, so that you are able to deal with changes when they come along. Inevitably, when you become more familiar with your market, you will find that you have to update your goals or modify the plans that you have put in place so that you are successful. Build you brand by leaving room to take advantages of any opportunities that present themselves to your business in the short run.

Build Up a Website

If you want to have a successful brand, a major part of your strategy should be on creating an excellent website. This is the most essential tool that you need when looking at brand development. This is where your target audience will learn everything that you have to offer, the methodology that you prefer to use, and who you are looking to target and fulfill needs. Even though your website may not be the only tool that is used to make a decision, it may be used to rule you out, particularly if it is unattractive or the message within it is wrong.

The first step is all about planning and understanding what you stand for. Take the time to do a thorough job and once you are clear about what your brand will represent, and how you will move it forward in the long run, then you are ready to move forward to the second step for brand building.

Chapter 2:
The Second Step –
Giving your Brand a Personality

Take a moment and visualize your relationships with your closest friend. There is something about them that you love, perhaps it is the way that you interact when you are together, or how you know without words that you can trust in them. It may even be something that you cannot put in to words, but no matter what angle you approach your analysis of your relationship from, their personality will play a big role in the bond that you have.

The personality of your brand is what your customers will be able to relate to, and what will develop your brand equity. Brand equity is the commercial value that your brand is able to get based on the perception of your customers. This rarely relates to what the brand can do itself, it is more about how the customer sees the brand.

Consider the sports brand Nike. What is its personality to you? It is likely that you will make an association in your mind with fitness and helping you to achieve your goals for better health and wellbeing. It also helps you believe that you can overcome the barriers that are in the way of you achieving your goals, that you can trust in the product for success.

This is because over time, the brand has mastered how to create associative characteristics that help to shape the way you feel about it.

Your Brand Story

To begin building your brand personality, you need to have a story that talks about your brand. In this story, you describe your passion for the brand and how you would describe your brand to another person. What do you stand for, and what do you hope to achieve?

In communicating your brand and building your personality, the message in your story needs to be sincere, as this will make it easier for others to believe in your brand. It should also create excitement about the brand so that people are willing to try it out and interact with it in various ways. These are the basic traits that your brand personality should embody.

When your customer is defining the personality of your brand, it is essential that they use a positive word to do so, so that your bland can continue to grow upwards. When negative words are used, then you can destroy all your efforts even before you have begun. From the personality, you can go deeper into building your brand and work on the image that you want to portray.

Your Brand Image

Your brand image is a part of a large equation that is referred to as your brand identity. Where the personality of your brand will address the emotional aspects of your brand and how a customer creates a personal connection, the identity is all about the image of your brand, which is the physical part of your brand. You will need to create visual effects such as a logo and have company colors that communicate what your brand stand for. It is these images that will be placed on anything that will visually represent your brand, particularly on marketing messages that are to appear on print, television, the internet or on video.

When creating your image, the colors you use are a tool for communication. They let your customer know whether your brand represents something happy, feminine, inviting or mysterious. Using a color like beige does not communicate anything at all. However, the color blue relays calms and professionalism.

The way that you use colors is also important. Creating contrasts with bright colors gives the impression that your brand is bold and can make a powerful impact. Warm colors will stimulate your customer when they look at your brand, and cool colors will leave you feeling serene. Colors which complement each other communicate that you can be trusted, and simple neutral colors display minimalism and simplicity.

The same applies to the fonts that you use when creating your brand image. Fonts like Times New Roman and Arial give the impression that your brand is organized and plays by the rules. Other fonts such as Comic Sans are light hearted.

Just like colors, the fonts that you use and the way that you use them will communicate something about the image of your brand. Should you choose to use uppercase letters, then you are saying that your brand is bold. Lowercase letters communicate informality, Fonts that resemble scripts and are curvaceous are more feminine and can communicate a special event or brand. The serif typefaces are those which you can trust and are mature.

Your brand may also use images within a logo. For example, think of the famous coffee brand Starbucks. In addition to making use of color and font, the logo has an image within it to attract more attention to the brand. When the images include squares, it is an indication that you are looking at a brand that is more formal. However, rounded edges communicate informality and a sense of fun.

Putting together all these differences is what helps to build a brand personality that can leave a lasting impression in the mind of the consumer. There is the benefit of an emotional connection as well as something physical for easier identification and reference. With this taken care of, it is possible to move forward to the next step which deals with everything to do with the customer.

Chapter 3:
The Third Step –
Focus on Your Customer

The customer is the driver of your business, as they control your overall sales and any growth that you can expect. Once the customer has bought into your brand, then you are headed for success. This means that you must find a way to include your customer in the process of brand building so that you are able to have a strong hold in the mind of the customer and in the market.

Famous celebrities and personalities have learnt of an excellent way to keep their customers invested in their brand, and that is by choosing to brand their customer. Sound confusing? Here are a few examples to elaborate. Singers such as Lady Gaga and Nicki Minaj have created special terms for their fans (who qualify as their customers). Lady Gaga refers to them as little monsters, while Nicki Minaj calls her fans Barbies. This creates an association that they can relate to, and makes them feel as though they are a part of an elite group of people.

Other celebrities have taken these names for the fans to the next level and used them on their own branded products. Consider the marketing driven family, the Kardashians, who have turned their entire family name into a brand. They have then used this name on a range of products from cosmetics, to clothing, to electronics and even publications. They call their customers dolls, and have taken this term forward to create more products and television shows that they customers can relate to. That is powerful branding.

Customers feel acknowledged and celebrated when they join the elite group of fans, and the same can happen for you should you choose to brand your customer. In addition, you should ensure that all the people that work for you, which means your employees are also branded with a name that represents what they do for your brand. This will help them form an identity as well, and strengthen their relations within your organization.

Interact Genuinely

Social networks like Twitter and Facebook have helped develop people and brands because they provide a platform for interaction in real time. If you want to build your brand, you need to master genuine interaction. This means that you treat each and every customer as an individual rather than a collective group. When you address them and their concerns, make sure that you use their names from the very beginning of the interaction that you have with them. Rather than using jargon, speak with your customer on online platforms as if you are speaking to them in person.

Give Out Points

The reason that you are working on building your brand is so that you can have loyal customers who will support your business by repeatedly coming back. It is much easier to maintain a loyal customer than it is to get yourself a new one. Creating customer loyalty can be done while you are building your brand by the establishment of a points programme.

With this type of programme, there is a simple formula that has been proven to be highly effective which should be employed. You will need to reward your customer, often with points, for every time that they interact with or use your points. Once they have accumulated a decent amount of points, then you can give them a valuable token. This means that when faced with a similar product that does not offer any rewards, they are more likely to choose your product so that they can benefit.

Offer Deals

Getting something for nothing, or making a saving will help to build your brand. This is especially essential when you are dealing with a customer who may have expressed some dissatisfaction with your services. When you are giving your response, make sure that it is fast, and also enthusiastic. Provide discounts or vouchers, or give them an offer that is too good for them to pass up. You can also use this brand building tactic to stay a step ahead of your competition. If customers notice that you are offering a better deal that those you are competing with, they are more likely to try your product and enjoy additional benefits.

Emphasize Care

Do not underestimate the power of customer care when it comes to building your brand. The best thing that you can do for your customers is to ensure that there is someone that is dedicated to meeting their needs, listening to their demands and serving them directly. This is so that you are able to strengthen any relationships that you have managed to build, and ensure that a connection remains between your brand and your customer. Reach out to your customer on a more personal basis, and resist the urge to rely heavily on electronic sources.

Keep it Honest

Customers prefer to interact and deal with brands that have proven themselves to be transparent in their dealings. When you are transparent, you are elevating the level of trust between you and your customer, and showing them that you appreciate their feedback. It is also an indication that you are doing what you promised you would do. This goes down to providing transparent information on their orders and showing that you have nothing to hide. It also indicates that your employees are doing what they are supposed to. The best way that you can build your brand by keeping it honest is to spend time having conversations with your customers on a regular basis.

The next stage of honesty lies in delivery. You will be making promises to your potential customers, including promises on delivery, promises on price and so on. Make sure that you work with integrity and are always keeping your word. This will assure your customers that you are working in a dependable company. It will also help with the management of expectations, so that when goals are being put into place, you are able to do something that is realistic.

Show Your Appreciation

Your customers need to know that they are important to you, which means that you need to let them know how much you actually appreciate them. Take the time to thank them for doing business with you, and to always treat them with utmost kindness. Ensure that when you are saying thank you, you are not sending a generic message that is the same for all customers. After you have done this, you should make a follow up if it is permissible to ensure that their needs continue to be met and they come back for repeat business.

With your customer on your side, your brand has its roots firmly in the ground, and it becomes much easier to move forward and work towards attaining excellent growth. Now you have probably started to create all sorts of marketing messages to encourage other people to try out your brand. This is so that you can get a stronger foothold within the market. The next step is all about ensuring you do this right so that you can enjoy the best results.

Chapter 4:
The Fourth Step –
Be Consistent in Every Way

It can be argued that the most popular soft drink in the world is Coca Cola. It has been around for decades and can be found in almost any country that you go to. There is something about the Coca Cola brand that you know you can count on, and if you are a fan of the brand, it is possible because you can trust in it. All this comes down to its consistency.

Being consistent applies to more than just the flavor from this example. In the case of a brand, it means that you are able to recognize the brand image anywhere, because the brand logos and color are the same no matter where you go. In addition, it also means that the message the brand gives out is relatable to what you understand about the brand. There should be no unpleasant surprises in store as you interact with the brand. Everything appears to be above board.

Consistency is important as it affects the way that your customers perceive your brand. You can say that it forms the tone of the message that you want to communicate. When there is a change in that tone, it is usually an indication that the company is facing an issue or making a move that has not been well thought out.

Looking back at the Coca Cola brand, there is an example that shows how being inconsistent, can ultimately cost your brand. A few years ago, someone at Coca Cola came up with an idea to create and market a new type of Coca Cola, one which was clear and transparent, with no color. In addition, the packaging for this product was not to be the iconic red, but to be blue instead.

When the launch of this new type of Coca Cola was done, it was a major flop amongst the customers, and some of the people who were consuming the normal Coca Cola chose to switch brands. This was all because there was a lack of consistency, and what the customers had become accustomed to was changed suddenly and without explanation.

At this juncture, the people who were in charge of the brand realized that if they wanted to further build the brand Coca Cola, they needed to stick with the principles that had been understood since its inception. Refreshment from thirst, the red color association, and the iconic logo that is recognizable on sight.

In another example, you can evaluate the way that the brand chooses to advertise in different countries. Typically, what happens is that the brand will come up with a global message, that can resonate in all the markets across the world. This message is the same everywhere, with the main differences coming in showing it culturally, as well as in the language that is used. What this creates are memorable brand campaigns that all customers are able to relate to, no matter where in the world they may be.

Consistency will make it easier for customers to relate to your brand, which is vital when building your brand. Moving beyond consistency calls for you to leave a lasting and memorable impression in the mind of the customer. That is what the next step embodies.

Chapter 5:
The Fifth Step –
Have a Creative Advantage

Creativity is the best way to separate your brand from all other brands that exist in the market. In fact, when building your brand and creating an excellent reputation, the best thing that you can do is be as creative as possible through the entire process. Creative brands always find ways to bring something new to the table, even after they have been in the market for years. They also get customers to interact with them in excitement as they do things that are outside the box.

Think about the brands that are in the airline industry. Which brand would you say is most creative? Following some deliberation and thought, one of the brands that is sure to stand out for its creative genius is the Virgin brand. This is because the brand is always coming up with new and interesting ways to communicate its offerings with the clientele. Whether it is through advertisements that are new to the industry like hiding an advert inside a job listing on a social media site, or creating an in-flight video that features dance and creativity to get the message across, this is one brand that goes the extra mile to separate itself from the competition.

The benefit of being creative is that your customers are always looking for new ways in which they can interact with the brand, and you can then take advantage of viral market to its highest extent. Viral marketing occurs when people start to talk about your brand, and you are promoted rapidly using word of mouth than any other medium. In brand building, having this type of momentum can elevate you to the next level.

With a creative advantage, you can build your brand with viral campaigns back to back. In addition to being highly effective, it is also low in cost as you are not paying other people to share the message for you. Often, you create the message that you want to share and the brand then picks up on its own.

Practical Creativity

Using creativity can be done in other ways, expanding on creating a campaign that people talk about. You could attempt guerrilla tactics to build your brand, whereby, you send all sorts of subliminal messages to your customers. For example, you could have your logo placed on certain items, including packaging, various accessories like bag tags, and coasters. These can be given to your customers as rewards which will please them and ensure that they see your brand more often. When they do, they will consistently have your brand in mind which will make interaction more likely.

Experiential marketing is a great way to build your brand. It requires you to allow the customer to interact with the brand before making a purchase, therefore, their decision to buy will be based on the experience that they have had with the brand. This minimizes the risk for them and makes the buyer more willing to purchase the product as they know that they will have no regrets.

Think Outside the Box

When you are marketing a product, for example a hair product, you do not need to use a hard hitting direct message to get your customers. You can play on different experiences that the target audience find relatable, and then send a subliminal message that connects to your brand.

For example, consider that you are working at building a brand that sells hair dye. In your communication, you reveal a woman who is standing in the rain after using your product, and she does not have an umbrella. As the rain falls all over her, there is no evidence that the color is running or fading in any way. This is not a message that says, I am building my brand by ensuring that you purchase it with this information, rather, it is a way that you get the customer to create a connection. By putting two and two together, it becomes clear that your brand is solving a problem.

With a creative advantage, you can now try out practical ways to interact with your customers, by ensuring the message that is sent out is able to reach them wherever they are. This leads us to the next step, which is all about using the power of modern media.

Chapter 6:
The Sixth Step –
Utilize Social Media

Part of building your brand is ensuring that you develop a strong brand presence, and the best way to do this is to be reachable to your customers, no matter where they may be. In the past, it was enough to use what were known as traditional marketing techniques, where there was emphasis placed on using print advertising, the television and radio to get a message to your customers.

There was no guarantee that the message relayed would reach the customer, and all that was depended on was a calculated guess as to the number of people who would interact with the product.

Technology has changed all this, and now it is even easier to reach your customer directly. To build you brand, you need to have a presence on the internet, and you begin by purchasing a domain name. The domain name should be the same or closely linked to the name of your brand, as when people are looking for you online, they will start off by conducting a search of your brand name. From this domain name, create an interactive website, where your customers are able to get information about what your brand stands for, and where possible, can also carry out purchases directly from your site.

To keep people coming back to your website, you must ensure that it is not static. This will require you to consistently update it, preferably with a casual blog that talks about your product from the perspective of the customer. This way, you can provide information about your product without actually telling a customer to go out and buy it, a move that actually puts some customers off.

The blog that you have can be updated once in a week, and can also include bright pictures and informative videos to attract and retain the attention of your customers. This blog needs to remain on topic, and so you should ensure that every article or entry that is featured directly relates to your brand, and possibly, encourages the customers to make a purchase.

To ensure that you have people reading the quality content that you have on your blog, you must take advantage of social media in a big way.

Social Media for Brand Building

People spend more time on social media that generally surfing the internet for information in modern times. This is because they can find everything that they need on social media, and it is friendlier, more realistic, and therefore, the customer trusts this more. There are thousands of social media sites that exist, but you want to ensure that your brand is present on the most popular sites in the world. When a customer carries out a search and finds your brand on social media, your brand becomes more credible, and it is also easier for them to share this information with other customers who may be interested. You also have the benefit of enjoying social media for free, though you can choose to pay nominal charges for highly effective marketing campaigns. The most popular sites to create a brand presence include: -

Facebook

This is the largest social media site in the world and it currently has more than one billion users from all over the world. On average, people who have an account on Facebook will spend at least one hour each day, interacting with other people and finding information. The advertising that is done on Facebook is carefully directed towards the right customers, based on selection criteria that is chosen when the advert is placed. This means that your advert on Facebook has a better chance of reaching the right person, compared to a billboard or a flyer.

In addition, you can redirect people to your blog or website using a Facebook advertisement. This allows people that may have never heard of your brand the chance to interact with your brand. In addition, you can create a page for your brand and gather followers, who are able to leave reviews, let you know their concerns, and get direct information on special offers or promotions for the brand.

Twitter

This is the second most popular social media site globally, and it allows for brands and people to directly interact with customers using short messages. There are currently in excess of 900 million people who have an account on twitter. On this site you can build your brand by using catchphrases or statements that will drive people towards your brand. It also enables you to get direct feedback from your customers in record time, which is excellent when you are working on improving your standards. Having a presence on twitter is appreciated by customers and will help the strength of your brand as it shows that you are willing to be held accountable for anything that is happening with your brand.

LinkedIn

This is a specialized social media site that looks to connect professionals with businesses. It is an excellent site to have a presence on as you will need to link up with other businesses for your brand to flourish, as well as people who are looking for a brand that delivers what it promises. On this site, you can create a page that links to your blog, where you share insightful information about your brand. Discerning customers will appreciate the effort it takes to maintain a page on a professional social media site, and are more likely to try your brand, and hopefully become loyal. The pool of members currently numbers around 396 million.

Chapter 7:
The Seventh Step –
The Long Term Growth of your Brand

From social media and all the other steps, you will be ready to target long term growth for your brand. The best way that you can do this is by building up your customer base. Brands survive because customers appreciate them, and through this appreciation, promote them in different ways. One of the best ways brands are promoted is through word of mouth, where a customer casually shares their positive experiences with others.

In addition, do not be too quick to outsource your brand building or marketing to another party that you believe could be more qualified or better able to do the job. The best brands have passion behind them, and this passion carries them into a bright future. The only person that can keep this passion growing is the owner of the brand, or rather, the person who has conceived. It. Therefore, it is essential that this person be the one to take care of the brand while it grows, and once it is built and has been well established, then it can be handed over to someone else to manage and elevate even further.

The biggest brands make strategic commitments to continuous development of their brand. Whether that means that they emphasize everything remaining the same, or thee periodically come up with new ideas to drive the brand forward, the process does not come to an end. As you begin building your brand, you need to understand that these seven steps are your starting point, and from this step going forth, you will continue to create more strategies to help drive your brand forward.

It is important to remember something though, the brand may change and advance, taking several forms over a period of years, but the product, particularly if it is a great product, should always remain the same. It is this that your customer is banking on, and essentially what they are buying when making a purchase. This is the deepest level of loyalty that you can achieve. If your customer is purchasing your product due to the marketing message, rather than the product itself, then you need to go back to the drawing board. Develop your brand more so that even in the absence of marketing, it is able to stay afloat with ease.

The brand that you build should provide you with several advantages in the long term, to guarantee growth. These include: -

- Being a worthy investment, so that any money that you put in to building the brand comes back in abundance.

- Managing the way that other perceive your brand, so that you communicate the right purpose, and that your brand is stable and trustworthy.

- Clearly communicate what the brands stands for, and the direction that the brand is moving towards.

- Stand out from the competition, so that it is not easy for customers to confuse your brand with another one that is similar in the same industry. This takes away from the overall value of your brand.

Chapter 8:
The Eight Step –
Tips for Success

Building a brand is a challenging thing, and it will take its toll if you are not doing things right. The best way to overcome the challenges that you may face in the process is with some amazing tips that will keep you going. This is a rapid way that you can achieve success, and build a brand that you are proud of. Here are the tips that you need.

Love What You Do

As you go through the process of building a brand, remember that you need to love the brand so that you can bring out the best of the brand. Have some knowledge about the brand, and this will help you apply ideas that will bring your brand to life. Along the way, be prepared for people who do not believe in what you are doing and want to bring down all of your plans. Do not let them achieve this. Instead, spend time fighting for your brand so that when others view you, they are also encouraged to interact with your brand in a powerful way.

Think Charity

Yes, your ultimate goal is to sell your product or service and make money, but when you want to attract potential clients, you need to reveal that you care for more than just their money. Find something that is philanthropic and commit your company to it. This reveals that as much as you make something, you are also willing to give back to the community so that your success is also the success of your society. Not only will this elevate your brand in the eyes of your customer, it will do the same in the eyes of your potential employees.

Fill up the Loopholes

As you are building your brand, you need to be clear about where you may not be very strong in the process. This means that you have to acknowledge that you have some weaknesses. By doing so, it becomes possible for you to resolve these issues and create a brand that is much more effective. Be transparent, and let your customers know that when something goes wrong, you will do everything necessary to make sure that you get it right.

Stay Professional

Making a great impression can be just what you need to propel your business forward, and you can do this by ensuring that you keep things highly professional. This comes from the look and feel of your business, as well as in your communication with your potential clients. Make sure that you use the best resources for this, as once you have established your brand, things will move more smoothly. Start off by ensuring that you have a leading marketer to push your brand to your chosen audience, and that you are making use of a professional website. Then, in your paper communication, have the same look and feel for all your staff. The professionalism that your treat your business with will affect the way that others view and perceive what you're doing.

Stay Focused

There are close to eight billion people in the world, but not all of them will be your ideal customer. Look at the market at large, and the find your preferred niche. Once you do so, you need to build your brand to ensure that you maintain loyalty. Do this by ensuring that the communication that you send out is cohesive and equal, so that whichever platform one is on, the message is the same. Keep your potential and actual customers up to date with what is happening in the business through a newsletter online.

More than Content

You are going through a journey, and when you tell someone about the steps, you will often notice their rapt attention. Why not do the same thing for your brand? Make use of infographics to explain what your brand is all about, and ensure that you have a system in place that will help you keep all the information close to you.

Begin your journey as a story, and get people to commit to the different parts of your story by providing them with accurate information. Make sure that it is exciting and you will find that your brand can grow faster than you imagine.

Building a brand can be thrilling, as long as you know the various shortcuts that will make the design process much easier. You should build your brand to stand the test of time, and create sales conversions for you. These tips will help you to achieve this and more. Remember, your customers are more likely to remain loyal to you, if every indication reveals that you are being loyal to your brand.

Conclusion

Are you now confident enough to build your own brand? You should be. Even though you have little experience in business or in marketing, by following these steps carefully, you will find that it is possible to build your own brand, and better yet, for that brand to be successful. The seven steps are all you need.

The first step requires you to have a strategy, take some time to plan the direction that you want to take your brand in. Then, you need to breathe life into your brand, by ensuring that you create a personality for it. This is followed by focusing on your customer, and finding ways to ensure that you get your customer to do the brand building for you.

This moves on to the next step, where you need to be consistent in everything that you do. Having a product or service that is reliable makes building a brand much easier, as you will be able to focus on your creativity. Being creative calls for you to think outside the box when it comes to communicating about your brand and all it represents.

To get the message to your customers, make use of social media which is a powerful force. Taking all this into consideration, the long term vision that you have for your brand will be easier to attain.

Elevate your brand with these seven steps, and you will experience success firsthand.

www.ingramcontent.com/pod-product-compliance
Lightning Source LLC
Chambersburg PA
CBHW070429190526
45169CB00003B/1475